CHAKRA AWAKENING

Guided Meditation for Chakra Healing, Chakra Balancing, and Chakra Cleansing

Sarah Rowland

Copyright © 2017 by Sarah Rowland

All rights reserved. No part of this book may be reproduced or transmitted in any form or by any means, electronic or mechanical, including photocopying, recording or by any information storage and retrieval system without written permission of the publisher, except for the inclusion of brief quotations in a review.

TABLE OF CONTENTS

INTRODUCTION 1

CHAPTER 1 *A Basic Understanding Of The Chakras Explained* 3

CHAPTER 2 *Balancing Your Root Chakra* 12

CHAPTER 3 *The Sacral Chakra and How to Navigate It* 21

CHAPTER 4 *Strengthening Your Solar Plexus Chakra* 32

CHAPTER 5 *Enlightening Compassion through Your Heart Chakra* 42

CHAPTER 6 *Finding Your Inner Voice Via the Throat Chakra* 53

CHAPTER 7 *How to Illuminate the Powers of the Third Eye Chakra* 62

CHAPTER 8 *Becoming One with Everything through the Crown Chakra* 71

CHAPTER 9 *Understanding the Benefits of a Strong Meditation Practice* 80

CHAPTER 10 *Ways to Align the Chakras Beyond Meditation* 86

Conclusion 93

INTRODUCTION

Congratulations on downloading your personal copy of *Chakra Awakening: Guided Meditation for Chakra Healing, Chakra Balancing, and Chakra Cleansing.* Thank you for doing so.

The following chapters are going to discuss the seven main chakra points in the body. Once you're able to understand why these chakra points are important, you will then be able to work towards fine-tuning these parts of the body. Developing habits that target these seven major chakra points will allow your body and your mind feel more intuitive, enlightened, and divine. Developing an awareness of your mind's eye and your spirit's sense of a higher consciousness will allow you to tap into your psychic awareness and sacred energy. Having a greater sense of your own being's chakra awareness will allow you to feel more vitalized and more open throughout your everyday life.

In addition to learning about what chakra energy can do for your body and mind, each chapter in this book will provide you with a guided meditation at the end of it. This way, you will be able to mindfully practice tuning into your chakra energy on your own schedule. There are many advantages that can come from meditating, and yet so many people pass up the opportunity to truly understand themselves, their environments, and their reality. Through greater mental clarity comes a happier and more confident self. This is why meditation is important.

There are plenty of books on this subject on the market, thanks again for choosing this one! Every effort was made to ensure it is full of as much useful information as possible, please enjoy!

CHAPTER 1
A Basic Understanding Of The Chakras Explained

Perhaps you already have a basic understanding of what a chakra is; however, you may also be in a situation where you don't know much about what a chakra is or what it does, yet you're certainly intrigued by the mysterious and seemingly spiritual nature of it. This chapter is going to seek to define the basic definition of a chakra. It will also get into why the chakras are important. Hopefully, this chapter will be able to prepare you for our deeper discussions on each of the seven main chakras that will follow once this chapter has been completed. In understanding basic chakra terminology and meaning, it should make the rest of the information that's presented in this book more accessible.

What is a Chakra?

While you may already know that a chakra can be defined as something in the body, it's important to understand that a chakra is much more than that. To start, let's unpack the word "chakra" itself. Chakra is a Sanskrit word. When translated, this word means "disk" or "wheel." Even though there are seven primary chakra points in the body, there are actually one-hundred and fourteen in total. This large number is suggestive of the fact that our bodies are comprised of many different sources of energy. Identifying the seven main chakras helps us as individuals target certain chakra centers in strategic ways that can lead to physical and mental betterment. The seven primary chakra points are also all located in places on the body where large organs, nervous systems, and psychological centers are located. This makes it even more important that our chakras remain open and healthy at all times.

The Endocrine Systems and Hormonal Balance

In addition to affecting many various aspects of our body's psychological makeup, chakra imbalance can also lead to hormonal discrepancies as well as lead to disruptions in the body's endocrine system. The endocrine system is comprised of all of the body's hormonal glands. These glands are monitored by the body's nervous system, which transmits and receives messages to and from the brain to the rest of the body. While there are many types of hormonal glands in the body, the most important aspects of the endocrine system include the following glands: the pituitary gland, the hypothalamus, the thyroid, the parathyroid, the pancreas, the reproductive glands, the pineal glands, and the adrenal glands. It's more than likely that you have heard of at least one of these glands before. Another primary reason why balancing the chakras is important is because without these centers of energy being in balance, the health of the human body is at stake.

What's Within a Chakra Wheel?

A chakra houses energy that's known as prana. Prana can be best defined as breath, but its definition is a bit more subtle than that. Prana is the cosmic breath of life. This type of breath transcends all layers of reality and connects the soul that's inside of the physical body with realms of consciousness that cannot be physically seen with the naked eye. Because prana is a vital life force, it's important that this energy is nourished through frequent and habitual chakra exercises. This allows the body in this world and the consciousness of all other realms of existence to stay healthy, awake, and in-tune with all that truly is.

How Do the Chakras Interact with One Another?

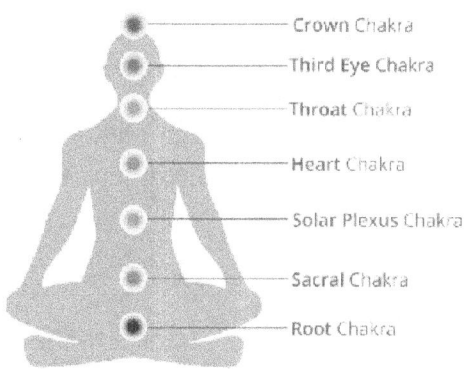

As you can see from the illustration above, the seven main chakras of the body are aligned directly in the body's center. This is one of the primary reasons why these seven areas of the body are considered the most important chakras in the body. In addition to being located in the center of the body, these chakra points are also all located along the body's spine. For this reason, when aligned and working with one another, greater spinal alignment is possible. Starting at the base of the spine, we see the root chakra. As we move up the body towards the head, we see the crown chakra. It's important to understand that the movement of prana throughout the body starts at the base of the spine at the root chakra. In other words, when you're working towards enlightenment and cleansing both the mind and the body, you are going to want to start by working on the root chakra.

It's also important to note that more often than not, only gurus have been known to have experienced an awareness that comes with having all seven chakras open simultaneously. The work that needs to be done within each one of these chakras is often complex and can require a significant amount of mental energy and awareness. That's not to say that your mind isn't capable of overcoming such feats, but gurus often dedicate their entire lives to becoming in touch with their various levels of consciousness and states of being. Often, it is not until a guru is in his older years of life that he is able to become completely balanced from a chakra standpoint. As individuals who are working towards chakra balance but also have other things going on in our lives, it may be realistic to only be able to clear out the sacral or solar plexus chakra in this lifetime. If you're looking at the chakras from a Hindu perspective, then this is okay. We have many other lives that we will lead, and we will be able to work towards opening up all of our other chakras in those lifetimes.

A Vegetarian Diet, Chakra Cleansing, and the 8 Limbed Path

You may not know this, but it is common for people who are interested in rejuvenating their natural and holistic internal energy to commit to a life of either vegetarianism or veganism. This idea not only stems from a desire to cleanse the body of all impurities but also has to do with the notion of non-violence. A major pillar of yoga philosophy, in particular, is known as the eight-limbed path. All eight of these limbs are supposed to guide a person towards a purer and more meaningful life. Without getting too detailed, the eight limbs of yoga are as follows:

1. **Yama:** There are five Yamas, which include the principles of nonviolence, honesty, unattachment, self-control, and not being greedy

2. **Niyama:** There are also five Niyamas, and they include keeping yourself physically clean, finding contentment with life, studying sacred texts (of your choosing), surrendering to your idea of God, and resisting the urge to be too flashy through dress or demeanor

3. **Asana:** Refers to having a physical yoga practice.

4. **Pranayama:** Developing the ability to control the breath

5. **Pratyahara:** The withdrawing of the senses

6. **Dharana:** Developing the ability to relieve yourself of all mental distractions

7. **Dhyana:** Frequent meditation

8. **Samadhi:** Cosmic understanding and complete integration with the universe

While all of these limbs are important from the perspective of cleansing and purifying the spirit, they can also be considered to be important from a chakra cleansing perspective for the same reasons. The first limb of the path, Yama, identifies nonviolence. This is largely interpreted to mean that in order to properly cleanse the spirit, a vegetarian or vegan diet is required. As with all of the other eight limbs on the eight limbed path, practice is required. This means that even if you're not currently a vegetarian, working towards living a vegetarian lifestyle is going to help to unclog all of seven main chakra points in the body. In this way, by living a life that is aligned with the principles of the eight limbed path, you will be constantly working together with greater chakra clarity.

CHAPTER 2
Balancing Your Root Chakra

Now that you have a basic understanding of what the chakras are, how they interact with one another, and why their balance is important to your body's health, we are now going to turn our attention to the first of the seven chakras. This is the root chakra. After reading this chapter, you will have a comprehensive understanding of not just what the root chakra is, but also how you can activate it. We will also go over colors and other associations that can be made with the root chakra in everyday life. The end of this chapter will provide you with a guided meditation to which you can refer as a way to open up the energy that is within this first chakra wheel.

Basic Information Regarding the Root Chakra

The root chakra is also known as the Muladhara chakra in Sanskrit. This energy center is located at the base of the spine, specifically where the pelvic floor is located. From a spinal perspective, the root chakra encompasses the first three spinal vertebrae. As this chakra is considered to be the first one, it might be convenient to think of it as the chakra of support or stability. In other words, the energy within this chakra relates to your sense of security in the world or the foundation from which you act. For example, food and water are both basic needs that a person must have in order for this chakra for being healthy. Some other basic needs that must be met in order for the energy within this chakra to be healthy include having a place to live, and feeling as if you are safe on a day-to-day basis. Fulfillment of these types of needs is often what stabilizes an individual, which often makes he or she feel less fear and feel more confident about their ability to thrive in life. For these reasons, the element that is most closely associated with the root chakra is Earth. Earth is what grounds our bodies to our physical experiences of the world, and it's also the one tangible element that connects us all other energetic beings.

It's important to understand that even if your basic needs are currently met, the energy within the root chakra is often energy that has been stored in your body since you were little. If when you were young, you often felt scared, emotionally unprotected, or otherwise unsafe, the residuals of this type of energy are likely still flowing through the root chakra. Often, the vitality of the root chakra has more to do with how we were raised and less to do with anything that we could have controlled on our own. In other words, if your parents nourished your livelihood and made you feel safe and protected on a consistent basis, the energy within your root chakra is going to be healthy. On the other hand, if your parents were not the most attentive, or deprived you of your basic needs as a child, you may have significant work to do on this particular chakra wheel due to blockages that were created in the past.

Red, the Muladhara's Color

Each chakra is represented by a different color. For the root chakra, this color is a vibrant red. Red is associated with the root chakra mainly because of the color's association with life, vibrancy, and ability to stimulate the eye. Specifically, the color red can be associated with the idea that help is needed or that action needs to be taken. For example, blood is red. One of the first signs that your body provides you with when you're cut or injured is of blood. Unless you act in a way that will stop the blood, you will continue bleeding. Stop signs and traffic lights are also red. These indicate that unless the appropriate action is taken while on the road, there is a possibility for an accident. This is why the root chakra is associated with the color red. If the energy within the root chakra is in turmoil, its energy is signaling for changes to be made in the hope that this energy can be restored to a healthier state.

The Endocrine System and the Root Chakra

Within the endocrine system, the root chakra is mainly associated with the adrenal gland. The hormones that are released when this gland is stimulated include ones that are secreted when the body activates its sympathetic nervous system. The sympathetic nervous system is also known as the system that is responsible for the body's fight or flight response. From the perspective of chakra energy alignment and physical body processes, this makes sense. If the energy within the root chakra is not balanced, then it's more likely that feelings that are associated with fear or insecurity will cause the body's sympathetic nervous system to activate.

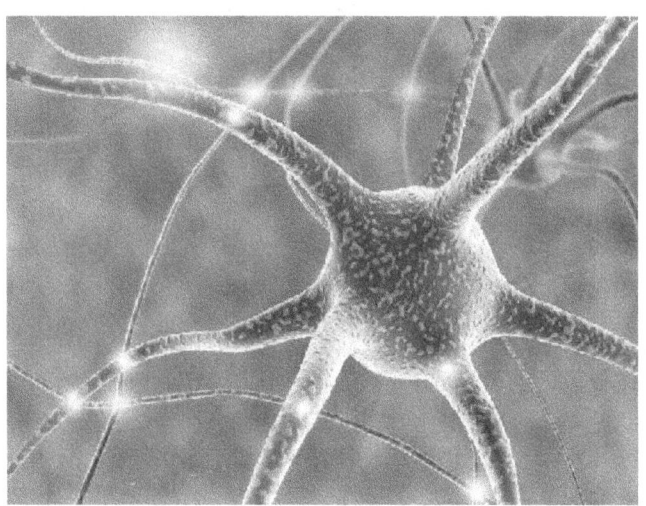

Your Emotions and the Root Chakra

Red can also be associated with anger or love. Both of these emotions can be found on the opposite ends of the root chakra spectrum. When this chakra is balanced, feelings of love towards the people and the world around us can seem easy. When this chakra is unbalanced, anger can often dominate the thought patterns of the mind. It's important to understand that anger is always a secondary emotion. When you're angry, there is always an underlying emotion that is disguising itself in anger. When the root chakra is balanced, you're going to find that you're less angry, more loving, and better able to express the emotions that are lying just beneath the surface of your anger.

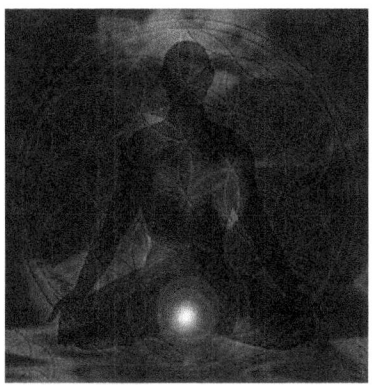

Symptoms of an Unbalanced Root Chakra

To figure out the current health of your root chakra, you'll want to think about whether or not you possess some or all of the following qualities:

- Excessive anxiety

- Suffer from nightmares frequently

- Colon problems

- Bladder issues including infections

- Prostate issues (in men)

- Feet, low back, or leg pain

If any of these issues are ones that are familiar to you, it's possible that you could benefit from practices that are related to root chakra healing.

How to Unclog the Root Chakra

Meditation is a great way to balance the root chakra, specifically because seated meditation in lotus pose grounds the body and reinforces the foundation properties that are desired within the root chakra channel. Other ways that you can seek to balance the root chakra include practicing Bandha yoga or chanting. For women, doing Kegel exercises will help to balance out the energy that exists within the root chakra.

Root Chakra Alignment Meditation

Meditation Duration: 5 minutes

Today we will be exploring the root chakra. The root chakra is located at the base of the spine and is the starting point for your chakra journey.

To begin, please seat yourself in a comfortable position. Gradually draw your focus to your breathing. Take a long inhalation through the nose, and a full exhalation through the mouth. Simply be aware of the breath, and take a few moments to allow your thoughts to slow.

I want you to imagine a beautiful, glowing deep crimson light at the base of your spine. Let it vibrate with a pleasant warmth. You are safe. You are secure. You are loved. You do not need to be anywhere else but in this present moment. The universe is supporting you, even as you sit here. There is enough for you in this life to live with true purpose.

Keep imagining this beautiful red light. Hold it there, until a sense of peace and security fills your entire body. Let the light radiate outward, into every limb, into every cell of your body. Feel the earth beneath you, supporting you.

Feel your foundation, strong. Trust that everything is in its place. Everything is as it should be. Continue to imagine this red light. When you're ready, and you have absorbed all of its wonderful energy, watch the light slowly dim. When you are ready, bring your awareness back to your breath, and to your physical body.

Slowly open your eyes when you feel ready, to end your meditation.

CHAPTER 3
The Sacral Chakra and How to Navigate It

Once you feel that you've been able to balance the energies that exist within the root chakra, you can then begin to focus on balancing the energies that exist within the sacral chakra. This chapter is going to provide you with information on what type of prana moves through the sacral chakra wheel. You're going to have a much easier time unpacking the sacral chakra energies if you take the time to clear the clutter that exists within the root chakra first; however, this does not mean that you *must* exclusively work on balancing the root chakra. Instead, when you first start to work on aligning the chakras, it might be a better idea to feel the types of energies that currently exist within each one in your own body. This way, you're able to sample the range of cosmic energy that exists within yourself.

Basic Information Regarding the Sacral Chakra

Also known as Svadishthana, the sacral chakra is located above the Muladhara chakra, and can specifically be located at between roughly two to three includes below your belly-button. From a spinal perspective, the sacral chakra is located at what's known as the lumbar vertebrae. To put it more simply, the sacral chakra is largely considered to be located in the pelvic region of the body. The prana within this chakra is the energy associated with how you perceive pleasure and enjoyment. You can compare this to the progression of a human life. When you're first born, you need your parental figures to provide you with basic human needs, which is where the root energy rests. Once an infant has been provided with these things, they then focus most of their energy on obtaining pleasure. Eating, drinking, sleeping, and occasionally playing can all be considered functions of an infant that are developed only after their basic needs are met.

The element that is associated with this particular chakra is water. Creativity, emotional awareness, and how we deal with intimacy are also all associated with this chakra. Water, therefore, is representative of the fluidity that should exist within this particular chakra. The sacral chakra energy emphasizes a need for the prana within it to flow without thought. This is done by developing an awareness of our feelings that may not be rational. Instead of acting in a way that is in adherence to societal rules and norms, our sacral chakra may desire us to act in ways that are more emotional in nature. This is the biggest obstacle that the energy within the sacral chakra faces.

Orange, the Svadisthana's Color

Ideally, the orange hue that is associated with the sacral chakra is a perfect blend of red and yellow. Not only is this color supposed to be a sign of strength; it is also supposed to signify respect for the nourishment of ourselves in both body and mind. This color is also meant to represent wisdom because the sacral chakra also contains energy that can hear your innermost voice. This voice is not simply the voice that you hear in your head when you're thinking to yourself. It's the voice that speaks to the piece of your soul that is connected to all realities and all energetic beings.

The Lymphatic System and the Sacral Chakra

Integral to the proper function of the body's immune system, the lymphatic system works with the circulatory system to carry lymph liquid to and from the heart. Lymph liquid is clear in color, which is another reason why the sacral chakra is associated with water. Lymph liquid carries white blood cells within it, making it important for your immune system. In addition to being associated with the lymphatic system, the sacral chakra is also associated with reproduction. The fluid and sensual energy found at this chakra allow an individual's reproductive organs to behave and attract similarly sensual beings.

Your Emotions and the Sacral Chakra The sacral chakra is the epicenter of our emotions. This chakra allows you to emotionally feel the world around you and opens the body to the enjoyment of life's everyday pleasures. Having good sacral energy allows you to think outside of the box, and nurture relationships in ways that are positive for your energetic body and your mental health as well. When the energy within the sacral chakra is healthily swirling in and around the pelvis, your ability to relate to others is going to expand, and you're going to find that your capacity to harness creative energy is going to become much stronger.

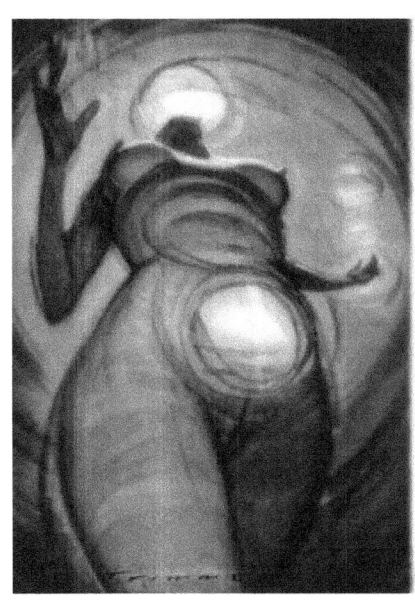

Symptoms of an Unbalanced Sacral Chakra

You'll know that your sacral energy could be more balanced if you can relate to any of the following circumstances:

You find that you easily attach yourself to others, especially to those people who can provide you with pleasure at a moment's notice

You're someone who often feels as if you don't know yourself. You are not in good touch with your emotions;

You engage in a lot of sexual activity, and often even fantasize about what your next sexual experience will be like or;

Instead of fantasizing about sexual exploits, you instead never desire sex and cannot be easily satisfied in that way.

When you're seeking to balance the sacral chakra, the goal should be to find a balance between the pleasure that your body naturally seeks, and the attachment that this type of pleasure can bring. If you're too indulgent or not indulgent enough, your relationships and relatability to others could suffer.

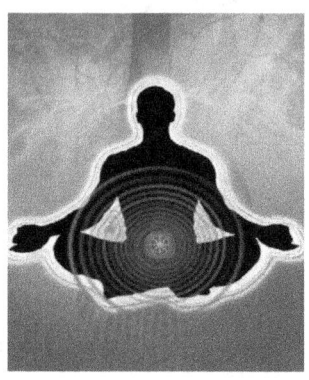

How to Unclog the Sacral Chakra

A few ways that you can rebalance the energy that exists within your sacral chakra include practicing certain yoga poses, dancing, and exercising. Hip opening yoga poses, in particular, are going to be helpful to the sacral chakra, since they target the pelvic region. Specifically, malasana pose, pigeon pose, and cow-face pose are all yoga poses that can be considered hip openers. Dancing is another way to balance the energy of the sacral chakra. This dancing should be spontaneous, fluid, and without thought. Exercising is also an effective way to balance the second chakra's energy, because of this chakra's relationship with the lymphatic system.

Sacral Chakra Meditation

Duration: 15 minutes

Welcome to a meditation dedicated to balancing the sacral chakra. Throughout this meditation, we're going to focus on reconnecting to our creative, emotional, and sexual selves. First, we're going to relax with a few deep breaths.

Slowly breathe in, allowing your belly to expand, followed by your chest so that the lungs are completely filled with air. Take about five seconds to do this. Now pause, and hold the breath for five seconds. Finally, slowly breathe out, over the course of five seconds, using the diaphragm to push out any remaining air. The length of time for each stage of breath is not important, as long it is done in equal measure. Repeat this process several times to deepen your relaxation. If you haven't already, begin to close the eyes.

Very good.

You may now allow your breath to return to its natural rhythm. We're now going to do a quick body scan, and identify any areas that may be feeling tension. Starting at the top of your head, mentally scan each part of your body, slowly making your way down to your feet and toes. As you find areas of tension, take a moment and breathe lightly into that area. Then, breathe out the tension. Allow this area to relax to its highest capacity at this moment. Then, move to the next area.

Finished? Great.

Your body should be in a state of complete relaxation. Next, bring all of your attention down to your lower abdomen, the location of the chakra. Acknowledge then release any distractions from your awareness, as you allow your sacral to become your sole focus as if nothing else matters.

With each inhale, imagine breathing bright orange light into your sacral chakra. This light is so powerful that it causes a circular current of energy throughout the sacral. Orange light swirls beautifully in a clockwise motion. With each out breath, I want you to imagine releasing any energy that is not in harmony with the sacral chakra. Refrain from consciously identifying the energy that you're releasing. Instead, set the intention to release anything that is not serving your highest good. Continue this process for a few more breaths. Breathe in orange light. Breathe out that which no longer serves you.

For each of the following affirmations, I want you to repeat after me, reciting what I say in your own mind.

I connect with myself as a sexual being.

I am passionate and outgoing.

I am liberated and able to express my emotions without being overbearing.

I express my emotions and sexuality in a healthy way and feel no guilt for this.

Because I connect with my true sensual desires, I no longer rely on artificial substitutes for pleasure.

I use my creativity to express my individuality, which is a Divine expression of the infinite whole.

I experience a fair and equal exchange of energy and love in all of my relationship.

I communicate my needs clearly, laying the groundwork for healthy relationships.

I respect and accept myself and others, exactly as they are.

I nurture those in need and accept help when I am in need.

You made it through. How do you feel? To which of those statements did you most relate? Which of those statements did you not quite relate? The goal is to fully connect with each one of those statements, as they possess innate qualities of our Divine selves. You can access any of these traits through your sacral energy.

At this time, I'd like you to imagine a bright orange wave, starting in your lower abdomen. A beautiful orange sea, which grows larger the more you focus on it. It now fills your entire abdomen, then your legs, thigh, arms, neck and finally your head. Imagine this wave washing away all energy that no longer serves your highest good.

We will close this exercise with a chant.

I will chant the sound "VAM" three times. I invite you to join me by taking a deep breath in and reciting the entire chant out. While chanting, think about the vibrations that your voice is making as you chant.

Take a deep breath in. Exhale completely, and on the inhale, we will chant together.

VAM. VAM. VAM.

Great job. Take a moment to sit and observe how you're feeling. Slowly let your awareness expand to y our immediate surroundings, as you return fully to your body. When you're ready, open your eyes. How do you feel now, compared to before the meditation? Did anything shift? This concludes our guided meditation on balancing the sacral chakra. Thank you, and Namaste.

CHAPTER 4
Strengthening Your Solar Plexus Chakra

With the foundation of the root chakra sturdy and the fluidity of the sacral chakra vibrant and moving, you will be ready to move on to cultivating power within the third main chakra of the body. This chakra is known as the solar plexus chakra. After reading this chapter, you will be able to identify the primary areas of the body that are influenced by the energy that exists within this chakra center. Similar to the other chakras that we've already discussed, we will also get into the colors and elements associated with the solar plexus chakra, as well as point out a few identifiers that can help you to strengthen and transform the energy into this space.

The Basics of the Solar Plexus Chakra

The solar plexus chakra point is located at the base of your body's diaphragm. In Sanskrit, it is also known as the Manipura chakra. The element that is associated with the Manipura chakra is fire. Prana, the breath, manifests from the diaphragm and provides the body with its vitality and ability to exist. Some sources also relate the solar plexus chakra to the sun, heat, or light. The energy within the solar plexus chakra, when moving and receptive, is able to attract other positive sources of prana to it. It's also this energy that provides us with the ability to think for ourselves, and truly take control of our own lives.

Yellow, the Manipura Chakra's Color

The Manipura chakra is yellow for a few reasons. First, the light of a fire often emanates a yellow hue. This represents the outward movement of the energy that exists within the solar plexus chakra. When your third chakra is healthy, you're able to feel more confident and get what you want from the world. Your energy will reach out towards your dharma, and you'll also be able to identify what your dharma with greater ease. Yellow can also be associated with the sun, the single most powerful star in our galaxy. Standing alone, the sun is strong without any assistance, and its light nourishes all energetic beings within its vicinity. The light of this chakra represents the strength and willpower within yourself.

The Digestive System and the Solar Plexus Chakra

In addition, to being located near the diaphragm, the solar plexus chakra also affects some other organs that relate to the digestive system. These include the pancreas, the liver, and the stomach. For this reason, one of the ways that you can maintain a healthy solar plexus chakra is through developing good digestive habits for yourself. Some tips on how to do this are provided below:

1. Instead of drinking liquid at a cold temperature, consider drinking them at room temperature instead

2. Avoid overeating when possible

3. Stay away from soda, fruit juice, alcohol, or any other types of liquid that are unnatural

Your Emotions and the Solar Plexus Chakra

By being attentive to the heat and friction that is integral to the energy in the solar plexus chakra, you are enabling yourself to develop a stronger identity and presence. Other qualities that will come when you nourish the energy in the solar plexus chakra include the ability to better discipline yourself, become more intelligent, and be able to form personal beliefs with more conviction. Nurturing the energy within the solar plexus chakra does not mean that you should become a narcissist; instead, you'll likely feel the ego becoming humbler because it doesn't need outside recognition in order to feel validated. When the ego is diminished, greater integration with the universe is possible.

Symptoms of an Unbalanced Solar Plexus Chakra

If you're exhibiting the following behavioral or psychological tendencies, it's likely that your solar plexus energy could be better balanced:

- You often seek to control your life's circumstances. You may consider yourself someone who micromanages or finds frustration in situations where you are not in total control

- You have plenty of goals and dreams, but you fail to execute these goals to fruition

- You are someone manipulative, or control situations to the point of deception

In contrast to the tendencies that were listed above, if your solar plexus chakra is in the balance, you will be more likely to be okay with changing circumstances or allowing someone else to take control of a situation every once in a while. You also may feel an effortless closeness with the world around you, because your solar plexus chakra allows you to feel strong, decisive, and confident without fault.

How to Unclog the Solar Plexus Chakra

In addition to keeping your digestive tract healthy and pure, there are a few other ways that you can seek to balance this important energy center. Since this chakra is closely connected to the breath and the diaphragm, breathing in a particular way can help to align this energy. To do this, find a comfortable seated position, and then begin to inhale sharply through the nose. On the exhale, breathe through the nose once again and direct the breath towards the lower part of your abdomen. While you're doing this, you should be focusing on engaging the stomach and pressing it towards the sacrum. Once you've become familiar with how the breath should be moving, consider quickening the pace of the breath. Inhale and exhale sharply through the nose, while focusing on engaging the core. This should feel like the abdomen is working considerably, even though you're sitting and breathing. The idea behind this type of breathing is to invigorate the abdomen and the sacral energy within it.

In yoga, boat pose (Navasana) and half lord of the fishes pose (Matysendrasana) both target the sacral chakra. Doing this pose is another way to ignite the fire that sits within this area of the body. Additionally, RAM (pronounced Rah-M) is the chant that is most closely associated with the sacral chakra. Repeating this chant before or after a meditation session is another way to balance this energy. Lastly, purchasing some yellow crystal gems can also help to bring awareness to the sacral chakra. By surrounding yourself with yellow or even golden light, this energy will be reminded of its illuminating capabilities.

Solar Plexus Chakra Meditation

Meditation Duration: 10 minutes

Throughout this guided meditation, we are going to focus on rebuilding our sense of confidence and personal power. To help ease you into a relaxed state, we will start with a few deep breaths. Slowly breathe in, allowing your belly to expand, followed by your chest, making sure to fill your lungs completely with air. Take about five seconds to do this. Next, hold the breath for five seconds. Finish by slowly breathing out over the course of five seconds. Repeat this process several times, to deepen your relaxation. If you've not already done so, please close your eyes.

You should be nice and relaxed now. Allow the breath to return to its natural rhythm. Now, begin to scan the body, looking for any areas of tension. Begin at the top of the head, and work towards the toes. If you find areas of tension, breathe lightly into that area. Repeat this process for any area of the body that is experiencing tension.

Have you relieved your tension? Good.

We're now going to place all of our attention on the solar plexus chakra, just below the navel. If there are any other distracting thoughts coming to your mind, acknowledge them, but then let them pass. With each breath, imagine breathing a golden light into the lower abdomen. Feel this color swirling amongst the energy within this area of the body. With each out breath, feel all other energies that are not serving your sacral chakra be released. Feel the body only filling with this bright yellow color.

Next, imagine that your entire body is becoming consumed by the golden light that is the sacral chakra energy. Feel this color taking over the lower abdomen, before consuming the chest, the shoulders, and the head. Feel this energy moving effortlessly throughout the body on each inhale and every exhale.

You are one with the sacral chakra. Turn your attention to these affirmations of respect for yourself in regards to the sacral chakra, and repeat these affirmations in your head:

I am in control of my life and live with a sense of dignity.

I use all of the information I have to make informed decisions in a timely fashion.

I use my personal power to help me expand and grow as a human being.

I am confident in the value I provide to others as a human being.

My logical brain knows exactly when to analyze a situation, and exactly when to let the heart take over.

I understand situations as they truly are, and know when to consult others when I cannot see the whole picture.

I feed my intellect and thirst for knowledge by reading, listening to others, and experiencing new things every day.

I use my logical mind to manifest my dreams and desires.

I am optimistic, creative, and respect myself fully.

I am comfortable with the fact that the only moment in which I have any control in this one.

I do not feel the need to control others, as I know that the only thing that I have control over is my reaction to the world around me.

Begin to notice the breath once more, feeling each inhale that you make, and each exhale that you make. When you feel ready, begin to gently open the eyes. Thank you for joining me for this meditation session meant to target the solar plexus chakra.

CHAPTER 5
Enlightening Compassion through Your Heart Chakra

With the power of the sacral chakra motivating you towards premeditated action and light, you will have a better sense of who you are and what your true purpose in life is. Your personality will likely become more vested in what personally matters to you in life, rather than what others find important. With your intention being less swayed, your heart will be primed to receive and send more compassion into the world. When this happens, it will then be time for you to turn inward and examine the body's fourth chakra, the heart chakra.

Basic Information Regarding the Heart Chakra

As you may already be able to guess, the heart chakra is located in the center of the chest. Even though your actual heart is located closer to the left side of the body, the heart chakra is centered rather than angled. The Sanskrit equivalent of the phrase heart chakra is Anahata. When the energy in the heart chakra is healthy and thriving, you're able to not just love others with more consistency, but you'll be able to love yourself in a greater capacity as well. The element associated with this chakra is air, as air is the element that connects our energy to all other energy in the world. The expansive nature of air is another reason why it's often related to the heart chakra. The heart chakra allows your spirit's energy to blossom, open and become receptive to love in all of its amazing forms.

Green, the Heart Chakra's Color

Even though many of us think of pink or red when we think of love, green is the color of the heart chakra because green is a color of growth. Plants of all kinds often have some type of green hue to them, and the often-limitless potential for natural elements to blossom and bloom is a primary reason why green represents our heart chakra. Ideally, this green is bright and calming, rather than extremely heavy or dark. Like the color of an emerald pulsating vibrancy to the eyes, the heart chakra sits in the center of the chest, radiating love, empathy, and compassion to all life forms in its path.

The Cardiovascular System and the Heart Chakra

The cardiovascular system is closely related to the heart chakra, and the thymus gland is as well. The thymus gland sits behind the heart and provides hormones to the body that aid in the production of T cells. It's also interesting to note that the thymus gland derives its name from the thyme leaf, which just so happens to be green in color. Transporting oxygen and nutrients to the body's blood and cells, the cardiovascular system is vital to the proper function of the body. The organs that make up the cardiovascular system are also heavily dependent on air in order to function properly, which can provide yet another reason as to why the heart chakra's element is air.

Emotions and the Heart Chakra

The heart chakra is often represented by two intersecting triangles. An illustration of this symbol can be seen below:

These intersecting triangles represent the fact that the heart chakra integrates all of the life's differences. For example, both male and female qualities cease to exist within the heart chakra. Integration is a key characteristic of this energy center, and the intersecting triangles are supposed to be representative of this integration. The heart chakra links the lower chakra points to the upper chakra points on the body, and thus allows for the continuity of the entire chakra system. Additionally, this Anahata energy also dictates your ability to truly see the beauty in every energetic creation on the planet. Through the expansive nature of this energy, it also allows you to experience relationships more fully, as well as limits the sometimes-overpowering nature of the ego by focusing the compassion within in us on other people instead of ourselves. **Symptoms of an Unbalanced Heart Chakra**

Signs of an unbalanced heart chakra include the following:

- Experiencing fierce feelings of jealousy towards what other people have

- Finding it hard to forgive someone, especially if it's for something that occurred long ago

- Finding it hard to be around other people. You spend a lot of time alone or even make up excuses as to why you can't spend time with other people

- You experience physical problems with your heart or have developed illnesses related to the lungs

- You're often overly defensive or have been described as argumentative

How to Unclog the Heart Chakra

If you do currently experience some of the symptoms that point to an unbalanced heart chakra, know that this energy can change and become healthier in nature. In fact, practicing how to foster better energy in the heart chakra can be internally as well as externally accomplished. To open the heart chakra, consider performing these effective techniques:

Notice More Beauty in The World

Each morning, consider five things for which you're thankful from the previous day. Doing this will force you to focus on the smaller details of life, and your heart chakra will be able to open.

1. **Perform Activities of Self-Care:** Performing activities related to self-care include coating the body with essential oils, and cleaning the body in a disciplined manner. While this may not seem like it will open the heart, this will allow you to pay attention to being attentive to the amazing vehicle for life that you've been given. This will also allow you to accept yourself as you are.

2. **Give or Take:** Try and recognize the type of person that you are in a relationship. If you're someone who typically gives more than they receive, then try and overhaul this behavior. Instead of constantly giving,

why not see what happens when you receive instead? If you're someone who typically receives more in a relationship than gives, try to do the opposite.

3. **Do Yoga:** Heart opening yoga poses include cobra pose, eagle pose, camel pose, and fish pose.

Heart Chakra Meditation

Meditation Duration: 30 minutes

Namaste. This meditation will focus on opening Anahata, the heart chakra. The heart chakra is the seed of love, compassion, and hope. First, we will start our meditation with deep breathing, before turning our attention to the energy that exists within the heart chakra.

I invite you to close your eyes. Take a deep breath, and then take a relaxing exhale. Let go, dissolve your problems of the day, your worries, and concerns. Come back to your beautiful body and soul. I invite you again to take a deep breath in, and then take a relaxing exhale. Release all of your tension on each exhale that you take. Repeat this for at least five full breaths.

You should now feel completely relaxed. Let all of the thoughts of the day disappear, my child of God. All that is left is your beautiful self. I invite you to take one more deep breath in, and then let it go completely on the exhale. Feel the tingle of coming back to the Self. This is your home, your physical temple.

This meditation will help to open your heart to give and receive the unconditional love that it deserves. Feel each breath entering the body like a wave on the ocean. On each exhale, feel this wave cleansing your spirit. Feel the breath, the sustainer of life, coming and going just like anything else in life. Continue to feel each breath enter the body, and on the exhale let go of any thoughts of "am I doing this right?" This is a space of Divine perfection, for you are perfect. Beyond it all, there's deep love within you, a love that has always been within you from the moment you were born. This divine love if yours to be discovered.

Follow your breath. Follow it into your temple. Exhale. On the next inhale, breathe in your heart's space. This is the sustainer of unconditional love. This is where all meet the light. Feel your heart. Take another deep inhale into your heart's space. Have every breath light up this area of the body. Another inhale, another exhale to your divine heart. I invite you to take another breath, into your heart's space. Feel green light coming in through the nostrils before illuminating the heart. Each breath should make the heart just a little bit brighter.

This is the light of our cosmos, of everything. Drink it on each inhale, and feel you becoming one with it on each exhale. You should now be completely relaxed and should feel able to enjoy a feeling of bliss and inner peace. Try to imagine the words that I'm saying, as they lull your heart into a space of complete and utter calm.

You are standing in a luscious field of grass, overlooking breathtaking mountains on a refreshing fall morning. The radiance of the sun heats your face, your body, and is even able to make the energy within your heart glow. Feel this glowing and miraculous energy taking hold of you on the inhale. On the exhale, let it go. Next, feel the grass playfully rubbing against your bare feet. Listen to all of the sounds that nature is making, and remind yourself how remarkable these sounds are. You are home here because this is a place that allows you to feel happy and protected.

You're in no hurry. Keep yourself in the present moment. Notice the giant tree to your right. Walk towards it. Stand under it. Notice its leaves, it's sturdy trunk, its thick branches. Notice that this tree is bearing fruit. Take a piece of fruit from the tree. There's no need to hesitate. As you swallow the fruit, feel it passing down your throat. Allow it to sit in your stomach. This fruit possesses divine happiness. Allow this happiness to glow inside of you, and allow its aura to travel upwards towards your heart. Allow this sensation to spread across the chest.

This is how love feels. You are loved. You are protected. You are a divine presence. You are enough. There's no need to think. Instead, feel how this sensation radiates happiness and kindness throughout your entire body. Take another bite of your fruit, allowing yourself to maintain this sensation of pure and utter bliss. Feel where this energy is moving, without trying to direct it or control it.

Stay with these feelings for as long as you'd like. When you're ready, say goodbye to the tree that gave you the fruits of happiness. Say goodbye to the mountains, to the grass, and to the cool morning air. Begin to bring your awareness back to your breath. Feel each inhalation, and each exhalation. Whenever you would like to finish this meditation, you may do so. Before you get up, give yourself some time to adjust.

CHAPTER 6
Finding Your Inner Voice Via the Throat Chakra

Being able to find greater empathy and compassion for the people and situations that exist around you will undoubtedly lead to a more complex and humbler relationship with the world. When you focus your energy on harvesting love through every relationship and action that you take, your energy will be less focused on the egotistical events that are happening in your life. It will also lead to greater integration with those around you and will provide you with a greater sense of togetherness and fullness. Once your heart chakra has become balanced, it will then be time to move onto empowering the throat chakra. After reading this chapter, you will understand what the values of the throat chakra energy as, and will also know how to express this energy more fully.

Basic Information Regarding the Throat Chakra

In Sanskrit, the throat chakra is referred to as Vishudda. When translated, this word means pure. Located in the middle of the neck, the energy of the throat chakra emphasizes your communicative abilities and how you go about expressing yourself through sound. In fact, sound is this chakra's element. You might be thinking that a chakra point by the ears would be better suited for the element of sound, but this element is meant to represent this energy's ability to both hear and communicate the soul's innermost desires. In this way, the throat chakra goes beyond the simple auditory processes of the ears and is able to provide a voice for the entire energetic body instead.

Blue, Vishudda's Color

The color blue is representative of our ability to link with the divine. The throat chakra, when balanced, is able to provide the soul with a link to the greater power that connects all of us through its mystical energy. This is important to understand, especially when seeking to understand the true properties of this particular chakra. Even when the body and mind are still, the energy within the throat chakra can hear and feel the sounds that are being transmitted from elsewhere. Sound is able to send vibrations that are both auditory *and* visual, yet the human eye cannot see these visual frequencies. Instead, the throat chakra is able to tap into the energy that is being created from a divine source and can then translate these sounds to the rest of body.

The Thyroid and Other Physical Elements of the Throat Chakra The thyroid gland is the primary gland associated with the throat chakra. This gland is located in the neck. For example, in men, the thyroid gland sticks out from the body in the form of Adam's apple. This gland releases hormones that help to stabilize the body's metabolism, as well as ensures that the body is growing and developing in a healthy manner. Other physical parts of the body that relate to the throat chakra include the roof of the mouth, the neck, the shoulders, the jaw, and the tongue.

Your Emotions and the Throat Chakra

Unlike any of the other chakras that we've discussed up until this point, the energy within the throat chakra consists of elements that relate to what's known as the subtle body. The subtle body can be best described as your body's mystical elements. This body exists on a plane that cannot be seen by the human eye or through any type of scientific medium. This is the body that is clairvoyant and psychic. While you may not be consciously aware that this body exists within yourself, it exists within every energetic being, whether we are fully aware of it or not. The subtle body is incredibly difficult to tap into and typically will require a lifetime of dedicated practice to properly balance. This chakra is also considered to be the gatekeeper between the physical body chakras and the chakras that can be found in the head.

As you can see, the throat chakra provides the body with the potential to tap into multiple realities and wisdom. This a quality that none of the previous chakras can provide. In addition to this cosmic ability, the throat chakra still does mentally alter the physical body as well. Having a balanced throat chakra will ensure that you're able to express yourself in an honest and true manner. It will also help you to translate your ideas and creative thoughts into action, through communicating your thoughts effectively. Some of these abilities overlap with the abilities of the sacral chakra. You can think of the throat chakra as being able to fine-tune the energy that exists within the sacral chakra.

Symptoms of an Unbalanced Throat Chakra

An unbalanced throat chakra can lead to feelings that are both introverted and extroverted alike. Remember, for all seven of the primary chakras, balance is key. Your throat chakra needs to be better balanced if you're currently exhibiting any of these types of behaviors:

- You find that you talk too much or too little. You either need to be the center of attention or enjoy being the mouse in the room

- You find it hard to listen to other people's opinions, or you listen to other people's opinions so often that your voice is often lost in the shuffle

- You may have a hard time keeping secrets, or you may find it difficult to share information with others. This may cause you to be perceived as unnecessarily secretive

How to Unclog the Throat Chakra

If you're experiencing any of the difficulties that were just described, there are certain actions that you can take in an attempt to balance out the imbalances that are occurring within the throat chakra. Some of these methods include the following:

Singing: Any type of singing is considered beneficial to the throat chakra

Drinking Water: There are many studies that have been done suggesting that Americans, in particular, are dehydrated more often than not. Drinking more water than you currently do is considered healthy for the throat chakra

Meditating on Blue: People who meditate frequently and consider themselves to have a deep meditation practice will often state that they can see a blue glowing pearl while in their meditative state. One of the reasons why this might occur may be because of the divine properties that are known to be associated with the color blue. By thinking about blue, the energy within your throat chakra will be more likely to activate.

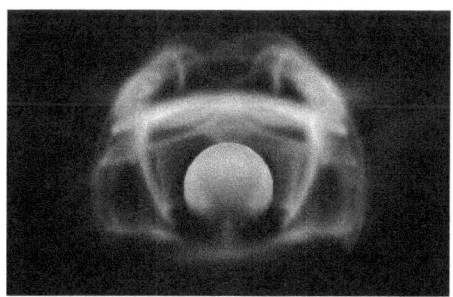

Throat Chakra Breathing Meditation

Meditation Duration: 5 minutes

Welcome, and Namaste. This meditation is going to focus breathing. Please begin by finding a comfortable seated position for yourself. It would be best if you were seated on the floor. From here, take an inhale, bend your knees, and place both of your feet on the floor. Feel the four corners of each foot firmly planting down. Take a moment to appreciate the supportive nature of the floor beneath you. Keep inhaling and exhaling in this position.

Next, place both of your hands on your belly. Inhale and exhale. Notice your belly filling up like a balloon on your inhale. On the exhaling, feel the belly releasing what it's holding onto. If you have not done so already, begin to close the eyes. Continue to consciously fill the belly up with, before letting it go. Do this for at least five breaths.

Once you've become comfortable with this type of breathing, on your next inhale, consider inhaling for five seconds. Count each second in your head. On the exhale, also count for five seconds, consciously allowing the breath to be released slowly and with care. Inhale. Exhale.

Begin to allow your breath to become normalized. You can let go of the count of five that you've been reciting in your head. There's no need to worry about anything. Slowly, bring your attention back to the room in which you find yourself. Wiggle your fingers and your toes. When it feels right, open the eyes. Take a moment to reflect on how your intuition may feel more expansive and open.

CHAPTER 7
How to Illuminate the Powers of the Third Eye Chakra

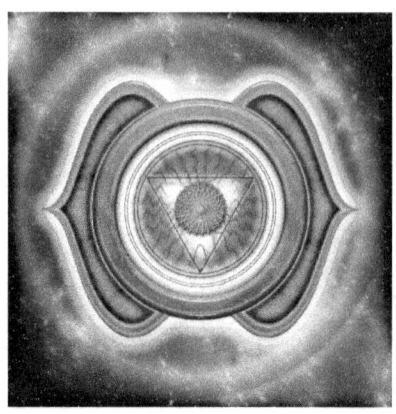

The third eye chakra may be the most popular chakra today. The intuitive powers of this chakra and the awareness that a balanced third eye chakra can bring to an individual is one of the reasons why it's so well-known and easily recognized. This chapter is going to look at what the third eye does, how it works with the throat chakra, and how you can begin to develop an acute awareness of the types of experiences that the energy from this chakra brings with it. Similar to the throat chakra, the third eye chakra is able to tap into the subtle body and intuitively see things that others who have an unbalanced third eye chakra cannot. The third eye chakra is an energy center that is mysterious, mystical, and intriguing simultaneously.

The Basics of the Third Eye Chakra

The third eye chakra is located between your two eyes, specifically in the middle of your forehead. The element that's associated with the third eye is light. Some also interpret the elements of the third eye to be a combination of all of the elements in their purest forms. Since the third eye is located between your other two eyes, the energy of this chakra is meant to be the mind's invisible eye. Its energy is motivated by imagination, purity, and complete freedom. In other words, someone who has opened his or her third eye chakra is said to be someone who is no longer bound to the mortal realm. Instead, this person's soul has been lifted into a state of being where the concept of time is obsolete. In Sanskrit, the third eye is referred to as the Ajna chakra.

Indigo, the Ajna Chakra's Color

As we've already discussed the throat chakra's color association is blue. We've already discussed that the throat chakra is the gatekeeper between the physical chakras of the body and the more subtle and cosmic chakras of the body. When we say that the third eye chakra's color is indigo, we're saying that its color is a deeper and purer version of the blue that is associated with the throat chakra. In this way, the third eye chakra is able to deepen the energy that is being experienced within the throat chakra. This ultimately leads to a more pronounced ability to tap into the subtle body, which in turn leads to freedom from the time-space continuum.

The Pineal Gland and the Third Eye Chakra

The gland that is most closely associated with the third eye chakra is the pineal gland. This gland primarily responsible for producing melatonin. Melatonin is a hormone that induces and regulates our sleep patterns. While that is the scientific way in which the pineal gland works, it is also largely understood that the pineal gland is the small part of the body that links the physical body to the spiritual realm of existence. This world is one that we cannot consciously see as humans, yet it is one that the energy within the third eye can access through the pineal gland's capabilities as a medium. The pineal gland is positioned in the center of the brain and is located in the vicinity of the brain's optic nerves. Its position in the brain causes it to be sensitive to changes in light, and some people hypothesize that this subtle awareness of change is what allows the pineal gland to tap into the mystical realm of the unknown.

Your Emotions and the Third Eye Chakra

While the other chakras of the body have distinct emotions that correspond to them, the third eye chakra is different. Emotions, in general, are sensations that only our versions of reality can experience. For this reason, there are not any specific emotions that are associated with the third eye chakra. When your third eye chakra is open and balanced, it means that you have become some embedded into the balance of the rest of the universe that you're able to recognize that your emotions are all related to attachments that your small self has to temporary things in your life. When someone's third eye chakra is open, they are likely going to involve themselves very little in the way in which they feel on a day-to-day basis. The recognition that all emotions are temporary, and that all states of being are always in flux, are concepts that are integral to an enlightened person's consciousness.

Instead, the third eye chakra is able to relay images to the brain that are difficult to verbally describe. These images can also be relayed to the brain as blurry images, rather than something that is extremely clear. When the third eye is able to capture these images, the idea is that your emotions are removed from the equation. Instead of thinking about these images through an emotional lens, the third eye chakra is able to look at these images through a lens that is wise and operates on a plane that is unknown to the likes of me or you. Your consciousness must evolve to a point where you no longer believe that your consciousness and sense of reality holds much significance. One way that this can be accomplished is through the denial and elimination of the ego. Only then, will true clairvoyance and psychic integration with the universe be possible.

Symptoms of an Unbalanced Third Eye Chakra

A few tendencies that can suggest that you have an unbalanced third eye chakra include the following:

- The inability to believe or complete rejection of any sense that there is another realm of existence or higher power

- Being able to only see the "important" tasks that you need to complete on a day-to-day basis, without any contemplation of the size of the universe or your small part in it

- You have frequent fantasies or are unable to differentiate the difference between reality and imagination. This can be an indication that your third eye chakra is overstimulated

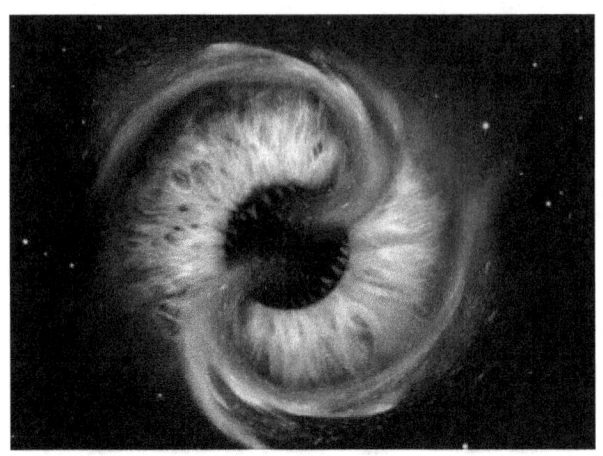

How to Unclog the Third Eye Chakra

We are going to get into the benefits of Reiki in a subsequent chapter, but participating in Reiki therapy is a great way to balance the third eye's energy. Placing certain essential oils on the third eye can also help to realign the third eye energy. Some of these oils include rosemary, sage, or marjoram. It's also been found that eating particular foods are good for the third eye as well. These foods include kale, blueberries, eggplants, plums, and sweet peppers. Finally, any yoga pose that emphasizes the mat being in contact with or close to the third eye can help to open and activate this energy. Some of these poses include child's pose and dolphin pose.

Third Eye Calming Meditation

Meditation Duration: 10 minutes

Welcome and Namaste. I'd like to invite you to find a comfortable seated position for yourself. Perhaps find a chair with a supportive back, or find a comfortable seated position on the floor.

Begin to close the eyes. Wherever your toes are depending on your position, start to focus on them. Begin to curl the toes and release them at your leisure. While you're doing this, perhaps turn your attention to the breath. Inhale your breath in, and see if you can imagine the energy of your breath moving into your toes. Try to only think about how this sensation feels, rather than focusing on any other thoughts that might be coming to the mind.

After you've taken some time to focus on moving your breath's energy to the toes, consider engaging the ankles, then the calves, then the knees, and then the thighs. Release this tension, and then begin to think about your breath moving through these areas of the body as it makes its way to your toes. Remember to also release any thoughts that might be coming to your mind.

Next, stiffen the glute muscles, and the pelvic muscles on an inhale. On the exhale, release this tension. Feel breath moving from the lungs to the hips, the glutes, and the pelvis. Relax. There is no tension here, no reason for stiffness.

Inhale, this time stiffening the shoulders by raising them towards your ears. On the exhale feel this tension release as your shoulders move back down the back. Feel your neck and jaw relax. Release any tension that you might be feeling in these areas.

Now that the entire body feels relaxed take a couple deeper inhales and exhales. Soak in this feeling of calm and serenity.

Slowly, begin to bring your awareness back to the room in which you find yourself. Are there any sounds that you notice? When you're ready, begin to open the eyes gently and become reacquainted with the space around you.

How do you feel?

CHAPTER 8
Becoming One with Everything through the Crown Chakra

The third eye chakra may be the most well-known chakra point on the body, but it is not the last chakra point that there is. The seventh and final chakra point on the body is known as the crown chakra. Similar to the throat and third eye chakras in the sense that it seeks enlightenment from a higher power, the crown chakra provides the soul with complete access to any and all realms of existence that are beyond this one. While the throat and third eye chakras can provide the soul with glimpses into the unknown, the crown chakra completely unifies our souls with everything. Think about that for a moment. *Everything*. Total integration with the universe has also been described as a state of eternal blissfulness or Nirvana.

Basic Information Regarding the Crown Chakra

In Sanskrit, the crown chakra best translates to the word "Sahasrara." Taken literally, Sahasrara means a thousand petals. The symbol for the crown chakra demonstrates this meaning. It is located at the crown of the head, slightly above the end of the forehead. This chakra allows the soul to identify all that is sacred in the world, and become one with it. It can provide the soul with ecstasy, bliss, and freedom from any and all patterns that exist in the world. For example, in some schools of religion, it's thought that our souls are reincarnated from one life into another after the physical body dies. From this school of thought, it's understood that when the crown chakra opens, the soul is no longer to go through the process of reincarnation. Instead, it will transcend all physical forms of consciousness, and become One with the universe.

Purple, the Sahasrara Chakra's Color

While purple is formally the color that is associated with the Sahasrara chakra, white is sometimes interchangeably used to describe this seventh chakra point. Purple is meant to signify connectedness, birth, and rejuvenation. Purple is also meant to signify a reconciling of all feelings of separateness within yourself and with others. In modern and ancient culture, purple is also often associated with distinction, wisdom, or royalty. A healthy crown chakra allows the mind to think deeply, curiously, and without limit. This is what the color purple represents, and why it is associated with the crown chakra. It's also interesting to note that all of the chakras that are found in the head are linked to similar color patterns.

The Pituitary Gland and the Crown Chakra

If you remember, the pituitary gland is responsible for controlling and maintaining the other glands that make up the endocrine system. It's located towards the base of the brain. Unlike the pineal gland which is located closer to the front and center of the brain, the pituitary gland is further from the mind's eye. This suggests that the crown chakra, while similar to the third eye chakra in a few ways, is far more interested in aligning its energy with the unimaginable and mystical than the third eye is.

Your Emotions and the Crown Chakra

One of the reasons why the crown chakra is considered to be the last primary chakra point on the body is because all other chakras must be in balance before this one can even think about opening. Now that you've learned about what it takes to balance all of the six other chakra points on the body, you can probably imagine that this is not an easy task to take on. When the crown chakra is open and flowing, it means that this energy is moving through all of the chakra points throughout the body. Prana is flowing freely, and this allows the body to remain in a state that is constantly rooted in the present moment. When your mind isn't busy thinking about the past and how it's influencing the present and the future, you're able to truly find a greater sense of freedom. Specifically, opening all of the chakras and finally opening the crown chakra will provide you with freedom from attachment, time, and ultimately the limiting aspects of your human form.

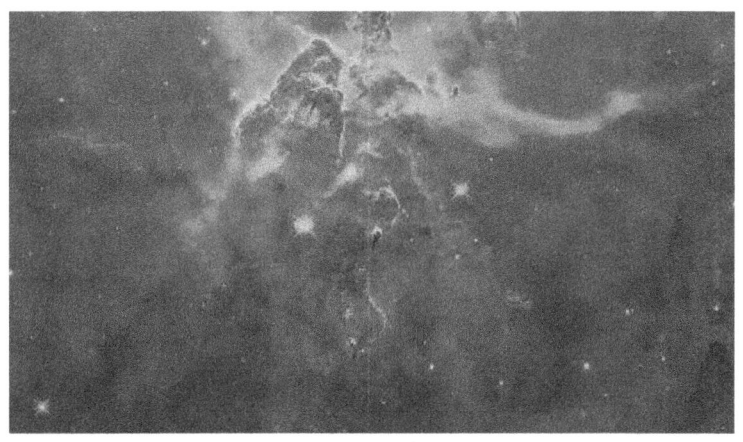

Symptoms of an Unbalanced Crown Chakra

An overactive crown chakra will likely exhibit this overzealousness in some of the following ways:

- Feeling completely disconnected from the body. You can't seem to relate to the physical body that you're in, and this leads to never being able to feel grounded in your own skin

- Keeping all of your thoughts in your head, rather than expressing them to other people

- Forgetting to take responsibility for things that are still important to your earthly existence, such as car payments or keeping appointments

On the other hand, an underactive crown chakra might manifest itself in the following ways:

- Having little or no direction in life

- Sensing an inability to set goals for yourself and see them through

- Developing nerve pain or neurological disorders of one kind or another

- Developing depression, schizophrenia or Alzheimer's disease

- Frequently experiencing headaches

How to Unclog the Crown Chakra

While unpacking the crown chakra to allow for a greater flow of energy is not necessarily easy, there are still plenty of habits that you can cultivate and practice in your daily life if you'd like to work towards that end. Firstly, chanting OM is a great way to stimulate the energy that is found in the crown chakra. You can either chant OM once, or you can also choose to chant it three times in a row. OM is a word that represents universal peace, and universal energy. It also represents a small piece of matter that exists within every energetic being and connects one of us to all of us. Chanting OM reminds us that our enemies and our friends alike all possess at least one piece of humanity that is exactly the same as ours. More importantly, chanting OM reminds us that there is a higher power, regardless of the exact form that it takes.

Crown Chakra Guided Meditation

Meditation Duration: 5 minutes

Find a comfortable seated position, and from here begin to close the eyes. Make sure that the space in which you find yourself feels calm and is free of any major distractions.

From here, take a large inhale. On the exhale, let all of the breath go audibly. Feel how this breathing brings a sense of relaxation with it. Continue this for at least five breaths.

Begin to think about yourself finding a greater sense of peace and focus. What would that feel like? How would that enhance your life? Begin to imagine what this type of life would look like. Allow your unconscious to bring these types of images to your head freely. What do you hear? What do you see? How do you feel?

Perhaps you already feel calmer or have a greater sense of peace in your heart.

Perhaps you can allow this sense of calm and peace to permeate your consciousness every day. Peacefulness feels good, and you deserve to feel good whenever possible. It really is this easy to find serenity in your life.

When you feel ready, begin to draw your awareness back to the space you're occupying. Begin to wiggle the fingers and the toes. When it feels right, open the eyes.

Did you learn anything new about yourself?

CHAPTER 9
Understanding the Benefits of a Strong Meditation Practice

Even if you're someone who feels like you're going to be stuck working on aligning the energy in your root chakra for eternity, this should not discourage you or deter you from developing a meditation practice for yourself. You never know what could potentially open up inside of you when you learn to sit and be okay with stillness in mind. Especially in today's society, our brains are constantly being assaulted with advertisements and social media posts that can cause us to feel less than content with ourselves. This is just one reason why developing a meditation practice can be beneficial to anyone. Regardless of whether you're someone who can only sit still for two minutes at a time, start there. Acknowledge and respect your personal limits, and work within these limits to find greater mental clarity, contentment, and inner peace.

Meditation is Scientifically Proven to Increase Happiness

While there has yet to be physical evidence of the energy within our chakras, it has been scientifically proven that meditation can increase a person's happiness. Not all people were created equal. It's been found that people who are pre-dispositioned for more happiness than other people have more brain activity happening in their frontal lobes. The term for your brain's natural state is known as its "set point." Everyone's set point is different. Additionally, people who are anxious on a regular basis have more activity on the right side of their brain. Studies have found that when people meditate, the activity of the brain moves back towards the frontal lobe, rather than to the right side. In other words, when you meditate on a regular basis, you are able to alter the set point for your brain. Even if you don't entirely believe in the powers that meditation can provide the body, this scientific evidence should entice you to at least attempt meditation to see if you're able to generate a greater feeling of contentment from it. Meditation should always be considered before medication is.

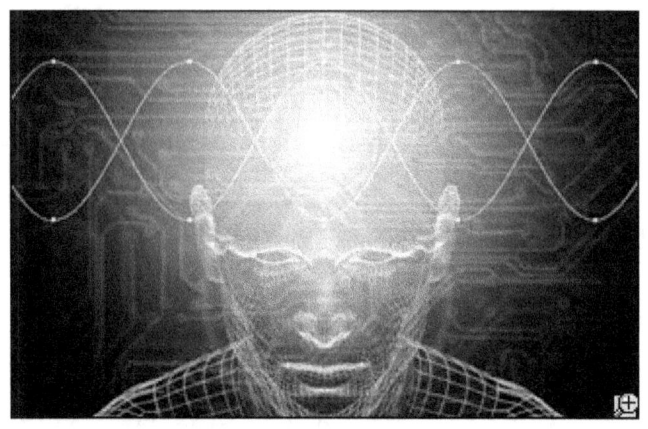

Meditation Makes Your Brain Bigger

In another study that was done, two types of people had their brains scanned and then compared. The first group of people was those who were dedicated meditators. The second group was those who did not meditate at all. What these brain scans found was that the people who meditated actually had larger brains than did the people who did not partake in a meditation practice. In another study that was conducted, it was found that older people who meditate on a regular basis have gray brain matter that deteriorates more slowly than those older folks who do not meditate. In other words, developing a healthy meditation practice can actually prevent your brain cells from dying. If this doesn't at least cause you consider meditating more often, then I'm not sure if anything will be able to convince you.

Meditation Helps Your Cardiovascular System

If you're someone who is worried about being at risk for a heart attack or other cardiovascular-related problems, know that meditation can help to alleviate problems associated with specifically your blood pressure. Studies have found that meditation physically reduces feelings of stress, and promotes feelings of relaxation. Specifically, meditation increases the amount of nitric oxide that the body produces. This expands the body's blood vessels, which ultimately causes the body's blood pressure to decrease. People who previously had issues with their blood pressure reported that after they started to meditate, their symptoms related to high pressure seemingly vanished.

Meditation Reduces Your Risk of Sickness

This book has gone into great detail regarding the types of biological systems that are influenced by your chakras. It's no surprise then that meditation has been proven to reduce an individual's chance of developing a common cold. If you're someone who typically develops a cold or the flu during a certain time of year, know that this type of sickness can be reversed through the powers of meditation. People who meditate are less likely to become sick and are also much less likely to develop sicknesses like a common cold. As you can see, when the mind is not cared for properly, the physical body will often pay for this neglect. Meditation forces you to take care of your mind, which in turn allows it to feel healthier and better integrated with the body entirely.

Meditation Can Help you Cope

Lastly, meditation can help an individual cope with any type of problem in life. If you're experiencing the death of a loved one, have been given the news that you have a particular illness, or are even going through some emotional strife, know that meditating is a great way to find a sense of peace and acceptance for the reality in which you find yourself. Turning inward not only allows you to accept the current and ever changing circumstances of your life; it allows opens you up to the possibilities of being able to forgive yourself and others.

As you can see, the benefits of meditation are not simply ones that can benefit for your mind for a temporary period of time. A disciplined and frequent meditation practice can influence both your mind and body both now and far into the future. The benefits of meditation are also not limited to just one area of your body or one area of your life. These benefits can extend and penetrate many aspects of your life, whether you consciously realize it or not. It would be a disservice to yourself to at least not even attempt meditating. You may come to find that meditation is exactly what you need in order to find greater happiness and a sense of fulfillment from the life you currently lead.

CHAPTER 10
Ways to Align the Chakras Beyond Meditation

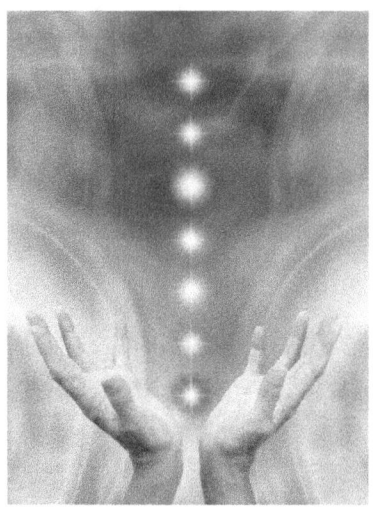

In addition to meditation, there are plenty of other methods that you can seek out that will help to release and activate your chakra energies within. This chapter is going to look at what you can do when you're already meditating and still would like to open your chakras in other ways. After reading this chapter, you will have many options when you're looking to open up any of your chakra energy centers. As you're going to see, many of these techniques are able to target the chakras in different ways. This means that not only will you have options when it comes to opening your chakras; you will also have variety in terms of how you're going about doing it.

Using Reiki to Align the Chakras

Reiki is a practice that's used to reduce stress in individuals and promotes optimal relaxation. When you attend a Reiki session, you are going to lay on a table, similar to how you would when you're getting a massage. Taken apart, the "Rei" in Reiki can be translated to mean "wisdom from a higher power," while the "Ki" can be translated to mean "life force" or "eternal energy." In other words, the point of Reiki is for the Reiki therapist to guide the energy of the individual towards greater harmony and alignment with the rest of the body. As you can see, Reiki has been known to directly influence the way in which chakra energy flows in the body.

When you're participating in a Reiki session, the therapist is not going to touch your physical body. Instead, you are going to close your eyes, and the instructor is going to place his or her hands on top of your main chakra points. These subtle placements of the hands over the body is able to positively influence the energy within. Many Reiki participants walk away from Reiki feeling revitalized, happier, and far more relaxed than when they first entered the healing room.

Using Aromatherapy to Align the Chakras

In addition to treating yourself to Reiki, another way that you can align your chakras is through aromatherapy techniques. In opposition to Reiki, aromatherapy emphasizes the physical placement of essential oils on the chakra centers of the body, in an attempt to reach the chakra topically. You can perform aromatherapy on yourself by simply rubbing a drop or two of an essential oil of your choosing over the area of the body where the chakra energy is located. Below you will find a list of essential oils that can be used when you're looking to target a specific chakra area of the body:

Chakra	Best Essential Oils
Root Chakra	Patchouli oil or rosewood oil

Sacral Chakra	Jasmine oil or sandalwood oil
Solar Plexus Chakra	Peppermint oil or cedarwood oil
Heart Chakra	Cypress oil or geranium oil
Third Eye Chakra	Lavender oil or marjoram oil
Crown Chakra	Myrrh oil or helichrysum oil

Using Crystal Healing to Align the Chakras

If Reiki and aromatherapy do not seem like chakra aligning avenues that you're interested in taking, you still have the option of aligning the chakras through crystal healing. Crystal healing is all about surrounding yourself with the color that is associated with the chakra that you're trying to open. We've already discussed the colors that are associated with each chakra along the length of the spine. When your eyes frequently see the color related to a certain chakra energy center, they're able to bring this stimulus to the energy that surrounds that chakra. Perhaps more significant, colors also have frequencies of light that travel along a wavelength.

When you use crystals as a way to balance the chakras, these wavelengths of energy are able to transcend the visual stimulus from the eyes and penetrate into the chakra in question. You can purchase crystal stones rather cheaply, although there are one out there that are on the more expensive side. Another technique that could be useful is to first surround yourself with the particular chakra color that you're trying to embody. Next, find a place where you can comfortably meditate. Next, meditate on the color that you've chosen. With the crystals around you and your mind focused on that color, you will be able to tap into the energies within your subtle body.

Using Yoga to Align the Chakras

Lastly, developing a yoga practice that focuses on the seven chakras is a fabulous way to get in touch with energy that is unbalanced or needs some awakening. Generally speaking, any yoga pose that requires sitting down is going to be good for the root chakra. This includes stretching. When you're trying to focus on any chakra point in relation to yoga, you're going to want to make sure that you're paying attention to doing poses that will utilize the spine in that specific chakra energy center whenever possible. You could also link certain poses together and create a flow for yourself that targets each chakra to some degree. Seek out yoga classes in your area that perhaps emphasize chakra healing. If you find a class like this, don't be afraid to ask the instructor questions regarding chakra balancing. He or she will likely have even more techniques that you can try out.

In conjunction with a chakra yoga practice, chanting is also a great way to target a specific chakra in the body. Chanting can be done at either the beginning or the end of a yoga session. OM, in particular, is a chant that can cause the body to feel complete and elation and bliss when spoken or sang. Another way to incorporate chants into your yoga or meditation practice is a mantra. A mantra is a phrase or group of words that are typically chanted in Sanskrit. Mantras can range from simple to complex and are known to be able to invite the spirits of the Hindu gods and goddesses into an individual's vicinity. Even if you don't believe in the Hindu gods and goddesses, chanting can still be a form of sound therapy for the body. OM is just one example of the many mantras that you can chant either on your own or in a group as a way to generate greater chakra abilities.

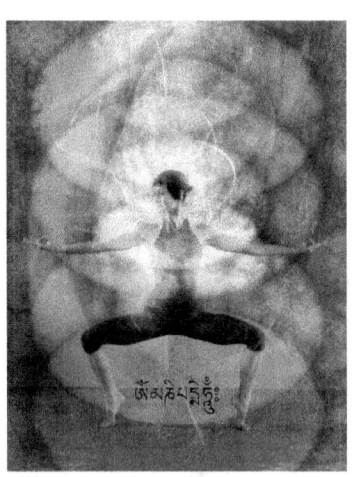

Conclusion

Thank you for making it through to the end of *Chakra Awakening: Guided Meditation for Chakra Healing, Chakra Balancing, and Chakra Cleansing.* Hopefully, this book has been able to provide you with the knowledge that will better integrate your mind and body. Remember, a key aspect of balancing all of your chakras is to start at the base of the body. Start with your root chakra, and then work your way towards enlightening the chakras that are closer to the crown of the head. When you're working each chakra point, remember to take some time to reflect on how your awareness of reality is changing and evolving through your chakra alignment work.

The next step is to begin developing a meditation practice for yourself. The guided meditations found in this book are a great place to start; however, you should also feel free to explore the nuances of meditation in any way that will suit you best. Even though meditation can certainly have traditional elements, there's nothing stopping you from making a meditation practice your own. When you alter and tweak the way in which you meditate when you're first starting out, you will be able to figure out what it is you like and what it is you don't like. This way, you will be able to develop a practice that is truly your own.

Finally, if you found this book useful in any way, a review on Amazon is always appreciated!

www.ingramcontent.com/pod-product-compliance
Lightning Source LLC
Chambersburg PA
CBHW071505070526
44578CB00001B/446